GARDEN DETAILS

DEDICATION

To my granddaughter and Kate's daughter, Abby Maya Thornell.
Her light shines so brightly; we can only feel joy in her presence.

ACKNOWLEDGMENTS

As with my first book, *The Hill Stations*, I worked with my daughter Kate on this project. There is lightness, joy and love in working with her and I want to thank her for what she brought to this book and how she adds to my life.

Big thanks to Mim Beaumont who helped me understand that gardens are an expression of our soul.

I also want to thank the garden owners, garden designers, horticulturalists and gardeners who have created the magic that I have been able to capture in these images.

Marg Thornell

GARDEN DETAILS
IDEAS. INSPIRATION. GREAT GARDEN SPACES

MARG THORNELL   KATE THORNELL

images
Publishing

Published in Australia in 2008 by
The Images Publishing Group Pty Ltd
ABN 89 059 734 431
6 Bastow Place, Mulgrave, Victoria 3170, Australia
Tel: +61 3 9561 5544 Fax: +61 3 9561 4860
books@imagespublishing.com
www.imagespublishing.com

Copyright © The Images Publishing Group Pty Ltd 2008
The Images Publishing Group Reference Number: 779

All rights reserved. Apart from any fair dealing for the purposes of private study, research, criticism or review as permitted under the Copyright Act, no part of this publication may be reproduced, stored in a retrieval system or transmitted in any form by any means, electronic, mechanical, photocopying, recording or otherwise, without the written permission of the publisher.

National Library of Australia Cataloguing-in-Publication entry:

Author: Thornell, Marg.
Title: Garden details / Marg Thornell and Kate Thornell.
Publisher: Mulgrave, Vic. : The Images Publishing Group, 2008.
ISBN: 978 1 86470 234 7 (hbk.)
Notes: Includes index.
Subjects: Gardens—Design.
             Gardening.
Other Authors/Contributors: Thornell, Kate.
Dewey Number: 712.6

Edited by Beth Browne
Designed by The Graphic Image Studio Pty Ltd, Mulgrave, Australia
www.tgis.com.au

Pre-publishing services by Splitting Image Colour Studio Pty Ltd, Australia
Printed by Everbest Printing Co. Ltd., in Hong Kong/China

IMAGES has included on its website a page for special notices in relation to this and our other publications. Please visit www.imagespublishing.com.

Every effort has been made to trace the original source of copyright material contained in this book. The publishers would be pleased to hear from copyright holders to rectify any errors or omissions.

The information and illustrations in this publication have been prepared and supplied by the author. While all reasonable efforts have been made to source the required information and ensure accuracy, the publishers do not, under any circumstances, accept responsibility for errors, omissions and representations express or implied.

Contents

Introduction	6
Colour	10
Foliage	28
Climbers	36
Borders	48
Stone	56
Structure	62
Art and sculpture	72
The formal garden	80
The cottage garden	90
The container garden	102
The contemporary garden	112
The artist's garden	122
The spiritual garden	132
The woodland garden	140
The kitchen garden	150
The water garden	160
The bog garden	170
The dry garden	180
The bulb garden	190
The summer garden	200
The autumn garden	212
The winter garden	224
The spring garden	236
Credits	248
Index	250

Introduction

$\mathcal{I}$t doesn't matter whether you are a complete novice in the garden or a professional landscape designer, you can always be inspired by what others have done. In fact there is probably nothing new under the sun in gardening, just new ways of using existing techniques! For centuries we have been borrowing ideas from those who came before us.

So where to turn if you are keen to make the most of your own space?

Obviously we can and should visit other people's gardens as often as we can. Open garden schemes have shown how popular this approach is. We can join a garden club and learn from those around us; these clubs are under-utilised assets. Or we can let someone else do all the hard work for us and sit in the comfort of our own armchairs as we are transported from one garden to the next by Marg Thornell's sumptuous photos.

You can use this book on many different levels, from browsing for inspiration with nothing particular in mind to a purposeful search to help with a particular project that you have on the drawing board. This is when the easy-to-follow topical chapters with their concise and useful tips and plant suggestions will come into their own.

You might want to be inspired by groups of plants put together well for foliage or floral impact or need to see how a well-constructed stone wall might look. Perhaps the artiste in you just needs some help to get the creative juices flowing, or you are at last going to put in the water feature you have longed for. Maybe you've realised that your garden lacks seasonal interest, or that your woodland has never worked and that you have never used or known how to display succulents well. Possibly you are hankering for the taste of home-grown veggies but want the patch to look good as well as supply for the table. This book will help on all these levels.

The photographs in this book stand on their own, but the useful lists, captions and suggestions add immeasurably to the usefulness of the book without bogging you down in the masses of technical detail already available to us all through the worthy and weighty tomes currently out there.

This is a book to enjoy and wallow in. In fact it could be just the very thing you need to own if you can't or don't ever wish to go out and get your hands dirty at all! Marg, Kate and the many owners of the gardens featured have done it all for us.

I hope it will, however, get you motivated to create for yourself the paradise you know you want and deserve. After all, the first paradise was a garden and we are all out there trying to find our own.

Stephen Ryan

Stephen Ryan started working in his father's nursery at the age of 10 and simultaneously joined the Mt. Macedon Horticultural Society. By the age of 19 he was president of the society and remains so to this day. He started his own nationally recognised nursery, Dicksonia Rare Plants, in 1980 and has been a passionate plant collector ever since.

Stephen writes articles for gardening magazines, has a regular radio slot with Melbourne's 3CR and does regular work with the ABC's *Gardening Australia* programme. He conducts lectures and seminars in Australia and overseas.

As a plant hunter and traveller Stephen has explored India, the United States, England, Ireland, South Africa, Peru, New Guinea, France and Argentina. He has also led tours in Madagascar.

Stephen has published two highly acclaimed books on rare plants and a nursery catalogue that contains more than 2000 plant entries, which has become a manual of rare plants available in temperate Australia. He also holds the national collections of *Cornus*, *Sambucus* and *Acanthus*.

Colour in the garden

*G*ardeners use colour in all parts of the garden to evoke different feelings and moods. Colour is also used to create impressions of distance and scale, to draw attention and to create beauty.

When using colour schemes to design a garden, there are many factors to be considered. Along with form and size, colour is one of the main contributors to a plant's role in a garden's composition. When a plant flowers, how long it flowers for and its foliage colour are all important factors when choosing a plant. The colour of the flower must also be carefully considered – not only by itself but also against its own foliage and surrounding background foliage. The impact of the flower colour can be subtly influenced by these factors. For example, a deep orange against a clear green background gives a fresh, sunny feeling, whereas the same orange against dark purple-brown foliage brings a more moody, passionate feel to a scheme.

The most effective borders use combinations of foliage and flower colours that seamlessly blend together in harmony or offer a delightful contrast in colour.

Contrasting colour schemes are at their most intense when they utilise colours that are directly opposite each other in the colour wheel. For this effect pair reds with greens, blues with oranges and yellows with purples.

Harmonious schemes are colour combinations that are easier on the eye and use colours that lie close to each other on the colour wheel. For harmonious schemes use oranges with golds, reds with scarlets, violets with purples as well as yellows with greens and reds with oranges.

COLOUR IN THE GARDEN

$\mathcal{D}$iscordant colour combinations can also work beautifully together, creating very individual moods in the garden.

COLOUR IN THE GARDEN

Colour sequences can change from week to week throughout the peak flowering season, as the different flowers bloom then fade. Careful planning must be undertaken to take advantage of these changes. What might start out as a soft-toned border in spring can become an intense, hot-toned border by midsummer.

Colour can also be used to create differing impressions of distance and scale in the garden. Cool colour schemes give garden beds an illusion of distance whereas warm or hot schemes shorten distances and can make spaces seem smaller and more intimate. Deep and intense shades of reds can be used to draw the eye in and therefore create a sense of shortened distance. To create a feeling of length in a garden bed, plant yellow flowering plants at the front and deep purples and blues towards the back.

COLOUR IN THE GARDEN

White flowers

Anemone hupehensis (Japanese windflower)
Anemone nemorosa 'Vestal' (wood anemone)
Campanula persicifolia 'Alba' (bellflower)
Clematis montana
Convallaria majalis (lily of the valley)
Cosmos bipinnatus 'Sonata White'
Dicentra spectabilis 'Alba' (bleeding heart)
Digitalis purpurea 'Alba' (foxglove)
Galtonia candicans
Helleborus niger [1]
Hydrangea arborescens 'Annabelle'
Hydrangea petiolaris (climbing hydrangea)
Hydrangea querciflora (oak leaf hydrangea)
Lavatera trimestris 'Mont Blanc'
Lilium candidum
Lobularia maritima (white alyssum)
Lupinus 'Polar Princess' (white lupin)
Magnolia stellata [2]
Nicotiana sylvestris (tobacco plant)
Nigella damascena 'Persian Jewels' (love-in-a-mist)
Phlox carolina 'Miss Lingard'
Polygonatum odoratum (Solomon's seal)
Rosa 'Iceberg'
Smilacina racemosa
Viburnum macrocephalum [3]
Viburnum plicatum [4]
Wisteria sinensis 'Alba'

Yellow flowers

Achillea 'Moonshine'
Aquilegia longissima
Coreopsis tinctorial
Coreopsis verticillata
Eranthis hyemalis
    (winter aconite) [1]
Erythronium pagoda [2]
Forsythia spp.
Helianthus spp. [3]
Hemerocallis citrina
    (day lily)
Iris pseudacorus
    (yellow flag iris)
Knifophia spp. [4]
Ligularia 'The Rocket' [5]
Primula bulleyana
Ranunculus ficaria 'Brazen Hussy' [6]
Rudbekia hirta
Tulipa 'Golden Apeldoorn'
Verbascum chaixii 'Gainsborough'

Orange flowers

Calendula 'Indian Prince'
Canna x generalis [1]
Crocosmia x crocosmiiflora [2]
Dahlia 'Biddenham Sunset'
Dahlia coccinea
Eremurus 'Cleopatra'
Erysimum wheeleri
Eschscholzia 'Inferno'
Eschscholzia 'Orange King'
  (California poppy)
Euphorbia griffithii 'Dixter' [3]
Helenium 'Waldtraut'
Leonotis leonurus

Lilium 'Fire King'
Lilium henryi
Meconopsis cambrica
  (Welsh poppy)
Papaver nudicaule 'Red Sails'
  (Iceland poppy)
Papaver orientale 'Harvest Moon'
  (oriental poppy)
Rosa 'Pat Austin' [4]
Tithonia rotundifolia 'Torch'
Tulipa 'Generaal de Wet'
Tulipa 'Queen of Sheba'
Zinnia 'Early Wonder Mixed'

Red flowers

Antirrhnium 'Liberty Crimson' (snapdragon)
Astilbe spp. [1]
Begonia 'Clips'
Camellia japonica 'Julia Drayton'
Canna x ehemanii
Crocosmia 'Lucifer'
Dahlia 'Bishop of Llandaff'
Dahlia 'Grenadier'
Dahlia 'Sure Thing'
Gladiolus 'Jo Wagenaar'
Hemerocallis 'Stafford' (day lily)
Knifophia spp. [2]
Lapageria rosea (Chilean bellflower) [3]
Lobelia cardinalis (cardinal flower)
Lychnis chalcedonica
Nerine 'Fothergilli Major' [4]
Papaver orientale 'Allegro Viva'
Papaver orientale 'Goliath'
Pelargonium spp. [5]
Rhododendron 'Elizabeth'
Ricinus communis 'Impala' (castor oil plant)
Rosa spp. [6]
Tropaeolum majus 'Empress of India' (nasturtium)
Tulipa 'Ile de France'
Tulipa sprengeri
Zinnia 'Envy'

Pink flowers

Aquilegia vulgaris 'Nora Barlow'
Astilbe spp. [1]
Astrantia major 'Roma'
Bellis perennis 'Pomponette'
Centranthus ruber (valerian)
Clematis spp. [2]
Consolida ambigua 'Rosamond' (larkspur)
Cosmos bipinnatus
Dahlia 'Lavender Athalie'
Dahlia 'Pearl of Heemstede'
Dianthus 'Doris'
Digitalis purpurea (foxglove)
Echinacea purpurea
Filipendula rubra
Lavatera Trimestris 'Silver Cup'
Phlox paniculate 'Skylight'
Polgonum bistorta 'Superbum'
Primula vulgaris [3]
Rhododendron 'Sir Edmund'
Rogersia pinnata 'Superba'
Sedum spp. [4]
Syringa 'Esther Staley' (lilac)

Purple flowers

Allium christophii [1]
Allium giganteum
Buddleja davidii 'Black Knight'
Campanula spp. [2]
Clematis 'Jackmanii'
Cobaea scandens
Consolida ambigua 'Imperial Series'
Dahlia 'Requiem'
Delphinium 'Black Knight'
Eupatorium purpureum [3]
Geranium himalayense 'Gravetye'
Iris 'Night Owl'
Iris ensata [4]
Liriope muscari [5]
Lupinus 'The Governor'
Lupinus 'Thundercloud'
Penstemon 'Raven'
Pulmonaria 'Lewis Palmer'
Salvia 'Purple Majesty'
Salvia viridis
Wisteria sinesis [6]

Blue flowers

Agapanthus campanulatus
Centaurea cyanus (cornflower)
Centaurea montana
Cerinthe major
Corydalis flexuosa
Delphinium elatum 'Blue Nile'
Echium spp. [1]
Eryngium alpinum
Hyacinthus 'Blue Magic'
Hydrangea macrophylla 'Blue Wave'
Hydrangea spp. [2]
Ipomoea purpurea (morning glory) [3]
Iris unguicularis (winter iris) [4]
Linum perenne (perennial flax)
Lithodora diffusa 'Grace Ward'
Meconopsis grandis
Muscari armeniacum (grape hyacinth) [5]
Nigella damascena (love-in-a-mist)
Salvia patens
Scilla spp.
Tradescantia 'Blue and Gold' (spiderwort)
Veronica prostrata (speedwell)
Veronica spicata

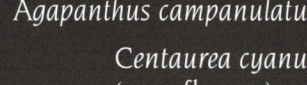

Black flowers

Angelica gigas [1]
Callistephus chinensis 'Lilliput Blue Moon'
Cosmos atrosanguineus (chocolate cosmos)
Dianthus barbatus 'Nigrescens'
Euphorbia dulcis 'Chameleon'
Fritillaria persica
Hemerocallis 'American Revolution'
Hemerocallis 'Meadow Sprite'
Iris chrysographes
Knautia macedonica

Nemophila menziesii 'Penny Black' (Californian bluebell)
Pennisetum glaucum 'Purple Majesty' (ornamental millet)
Rosa 'Nuits de Young'
Scabiosa atropurpurea 'Ace of Spades'
Sedum 'Purple Emperor' [2]
Tradescantia pallida [3]
Trillium chloropetalum [4]
Tulipa 'Black Parrot'
Tulipa 'Queen of the Night' [5]
Viola 'Roscastle Black'

Foliage

As significant as flowers in the garden and yet often overlooked is foliage. Foliage colour and form is much more important in creating successful lasting planting schemes than flowers. Foliage sets off flowers, disguises finishing bulbs and other plants and provides bulk and substance to a planting. The key feature of many plants is foliage rather than flower. The rodgersia, for example, is grown not for its pinkish flower but for the giant bronze leaves underneath.

Some of the most **outstanding** and dramatic foliage plants are the **silvers** and **greys**. They **harmonise** beautifully with many other colours and work well as a colour scheme on their own or mixed simply with whites. One of the most popular silver foliage plants is *Stachys byzantina* (lamb's ears), which **thrives** in most soils and looks glorious **mass planted** along the edge of borders. *Artemisia absinthium* (common wormwood), *Lavandula angustifolia* (English lavender), *Verbascum olympicum* and some salvias also offer great silver and grey **foliage choices**.

Deep purple and black foliage plants offer a wonderful contrast to work in with colour schemes. For good dark foliage you can't go past *Ophiopogon planiscapus* 'Nigrescens' (black mondo), *Phormium tenax* 'Purpureum', *Cotinus coggygria* 'Royal Purple', *Euphorbia dulcis* 'Chameleon' and *Cimicifuga simplex* 'Brunette'.

One should never overlook the decorative use of foliage with contrasting, variegated leaf colour. Variegated leaves can brighten and add dimension to dark and shady borders. There are many variegated grasses and the most interesting forms have striking variations such as M*iscanthus sinensis* 'Zebrinus' (zebra grass). Primarily grown for their foliage, hostas have variegations in golds, creams and whites.

Some varieties of shade lovers such as Brunnera macrophylla and pulmonarias as well as dogwoods (Cornus mas 'Variegata') and viburnums have striking variegations.

Plants for foliage

Aquilegia ssp. [1]
Ajuga reptans 'Catlin's Giant'
Artemisia absinthium
  (common wormwood)
Arum italicum 'Marmoratum'
  (Italian arum)
Berberis thunbergii 'Red Pillar'
Bergenia spp.
Canna spp. [2]
Cimicifuga simplex 'Brunette'
Cotinus coggygria 'Royal Purple'
Crocosmia 'Lucifer'
Cyclamen spp.
Dahlia 'Bishop of Llandaff'
Epimedium spp.
Euphorbia spp.
Gunnera manicata [3]
Heuchera spp.
Hosta spp. [4]
Imperator cylindrica rubra
  (Japanese blood grass) [5]
Lamium spp.

Lavandula angustifolia
  (English lavender)
Liriope muscari
  (lily turf)
Matteuccia struthiopteris
  (shuttlecock fern)
Melianthus major
Miscanthus sinensis 'Zebrinus'
  (zebra grass) [6]
Ophiopogon planiscapus 'Nigrescens'
  (black mondo)
Phormium tenax 'Purpureum'
  (New Zealand flax) [7]
Pulmonaria spp.
Rodgersia aesculifolia
Rodgersia pinnata
Sedum 'Autumn Joy'
Stachys byzantia
  (lamb's ears)
Tellima grandiflora spp.
Tiarella spp.
Tradescantia pallida [8]

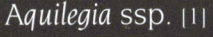

Climbers

Most climbers are used purely for their foliage and beautiful blooms, but they have other appealing features as well. Climbers are often fast growers and can offer an established look to a garden in no time. They can be used to conceal unsightly elements, such as tanks or garden sheds, or to screen and divide 'rooms' within a garden.

*C*limbers can soften the severe lines of buildings and arbours or create hidden and secret spaces within a garden. They work particularly well framing entries or providing privacy for smaller courtyards.

CLIMBERS

A common choice for pergolas and other outdoor areas around the house is the glorious *Vitis coignetiae*, more commonly known as the crimson glory vine. In summer it provides a welcome shady retreat from the hot sun; in autumn the glow and vibrancy of its colours in scarlet and orange provide a superb tapestry of colour; and in winter it loses its leaves to let in the warmth of the sun.

Another popular choice is wisteria, most famously known for gracing the bridge in Claude Monet's garden in Giverny.

Wisteria is a deciduous climber that blooms in early spring in white, blues and lilacs. Some wisteria blooms can reach up to a metre in length.

CLIMBERS

Clematis also provide a glorious flower choice. Their rich hues and varied blooming times allow a garden to be full of colour from late winter through to autumn.

Some climbers are used within gardens to spread throughout a bed among neighbouring plants, creating a more wild and rambling effect.

Beans and other climbing vegetables can be used in kitchen gardens to create points of interest and accents within garden beds, or simply to disguise composting and working areas. There are myriad uses and choices for gardening with climbers.

Climbers for the garden

Actinidia
(kiwifruit)

Akebia quinata
(chocolate vine)

Bougainvillea spp. [1]

Clematis montana [2]

Humulus lupulus
(hops)

Hydrangea petiolaris
(climbing hydrangea)

Ipomoea purpurea
(morning glory) [3]

Lapageria rosea
(Chilean bellflower) [4]

Lathyrus odoratus
(sweet pea)

Lonicera
(honeysuckle) [5]

Mandevilla sanderei
(Chilean jasmine)

Parthenocissus quinquefolia
(Virginia creeper) [6]

Parthenocissus tricuspidata
(Boston ivy)

Passiflora caerulae
(passionflowers)

Rosa spp.

Trachelospermum jasminoides
(star jasmine)

Vitis coignetiae
(crimson glory vine) [7]

Wisteria floribunda
(Japanese wisteria) [8]

Borders

Often unsurpassed for colour and drama in the garden is the flower border in summer. These borders are brought together with glorious colour schemes and although perennials play the integral role, shrubs, annuals and bulbs are also an invaluable addition.

The differing characteristics of plants are used to build the composition of the border, whether it is plant form, growth habit, size or colour. Plants should be used according to their attributes. Consider if they are key plants, good foliage plants or backdrop plants, ideal plants for massing, and if they suit the chosen colour scheme.

Clumping perennials that flower for long periods of time are key plants to plan around. Plant annuals in drifts to cover bare soil and hide any finishing bulbs.

Plants such as sedums and Japanese Anemones offer invaluable foliage choice for borders over summer and produce gorgeous flowers towards the end of the season and into autumn.

Perennials chosen for foliage colour offer wonderful backdrops for other neighbouring plants and provide the chance to exploit a large range of green shades as well as more dramatic variegations of yellows and whites, as well as a range of silvers, greys, bronzes and purples.

There is also the performance of a plant to consider – will a flower die back to produce wonderful seed heads to be enjoyed for weeks to come or will it rapidly disappear and become unsightly? These are all important factors to consider when planning a flower border.

For a more formal herbaceous border, the style is usually one of repetition planting using clumps of perennials, annuals and bulbs with a repeated colour scheme flowing through the border. The planting is usually planned with a layered effect from the back to the front. The mid-sized plants in the middle of the border join taller plants at the rear of the border to create the framework of the bed. The front of the border contains smaller edging or groundcover plants that complete this layering. There should always be slight variance in the planting to make sure the border never looks too contrived.

BORDERS

Stone

*A*ny garden can be beautifully enhanced with the use of stone, whether in decorative features or in walls and paths. Through careful selection and placement of feature rocks, you can develop a garden into an attractive, natural-looking landscape even if the plot has no existing natural features.

Rockeries and stone retaining walls can support soil and **prevent erosion** on sloping and uneven plots. Raised rockeries assist with drainage when using drought-tolerant plants such as alpines and succulents. **Tiered stone** retaining walls effectively contain garden beds on **steep slopes** and stone features add interest to a flat piece of land. **Pebbles** and **stones** are useful for creating traditional Buddhist Zen gardens.

Stone is an invaluable material when creating water features. It can be used to create natural-looking **streams** or **waterfalls**, or as a border to surround **reflection** pools. Stonemasons can create stunning **sculptures** from carved rock, incorporating **water features** into their creations.

Stone can be used to great effect in retaining and garden walls to achieve an appearance of age. By using moss- or lichen-covered fieldstone or reclaimed stone rather than newly quarried stone, it is easier to create

a mature-garden look and add instant character to period properties. This character will be further enhanced if the site is already blessed with mature trees.

Stone can lend itself to a more informal feel and stepping-stone paths and the age-old art of dry stone walling are perfect additions to the cottage or woodland garden. Whether your garden suits a flight

of weathered stone steps with self sown daisies cascading over the edges, or a Zen-inspired carved stone outcropping, you will always find a creative or practical use for stone.

Structure

A garden will always benefit from the addition of some form of decorative or functional structure, whether a whimsical shed, a romantic arbour or a simple timber chair.

A storage place for tools need not be purely functional; it is also an opportunity to create an architectural statement. You could create a whimsical little log cabin with a tin roof covered in flowering climbers, or an artful studio space with mosaics or other decorative features.

Arbours and pergolas come in many different shapes and sizes and may utilise various materials – from ornate wrought iron to natural rusted steel, painted or stained timbers to woven willow and hazel. Both arbours and pergolas will support flowering climbers.

Walkways and planted tunnels in a large garden can produce a delightful abundance of colour when in full bloom. On a smaller scale, a single arch holding a scented climbing rose will add elegance to a garden.

Gazebos are wonderful places to sit and contemplate the surroundings and fully appreciate the beauty of a garden. They also provide a great opportunity to create an outdoor eating area or BBQ area away from the house.

If space is limited, gates and fences are a perfect way to add dimension and mood to a garden. An ornate wrought-iron gate provides a glorious elegance to a garden. A woven willow fence offers the feeling of being in an untamed wonderland.

Seats, however constructed, are a welcome addition to any garden. They

provide a spot where one can linger and enjoy the sights and scents of the surroundings.

Timber or wrought-iron obelisks can give structure and accent to a border or kitchen garden, or simply frame an entrance or pathway.

Structures provide added interest, colour and texture to the garden. No matter what type of structure is chosen, it should be linked somehow to the composition of the garden and the forms of surrounding buildings and trees.

STRUCTURE

Art and sculpture

One is only limited by the imagination when it comes to decorating a garden. For centuries, beautiful pieces of art have decorated and defined formal gardens. From Roman marble statues to imposing bronze fountains, majestic urns atop stone pillars to hidden grottos, magnificent arbours trailing with climbers to ornate gates dividing garden rooms, each different piece provides a focal point, a hidden treasure or an accent that sets the style and tells the story of the garden.

There are no hard and fast rules as to what sculpture or art should grace our gardens. From wicker chairs to carved-stone water features, the tone of a garden is often set by the style of piece chosen.

The more **traditional** and formal gardens lend themselves to a classic look, perhaps incorporating the **graceful** lines of a stone bust, the **regal** touch of large lichen-covered **urns** framing an entrance or the simple **charm** of a baroque-style cherub.

ART AND SCULPTURE

The cottage garden has the advantage of suiting all manner of rustic treasures – from the artistic blend of recycled wire and wood used to create birdcages, mirror frames and other surprising pieces to quaint collections of vintage finds. Mosaic wall panels and seats in myriad colours complement mass plantings of bright colours in a cottage garden. An array of seating options can beautify any part of a garden. Colourful painted wicker chairs will look striking set among drifts of annuals in contrasting colours. Elaborate cast-iron furniture, slightly rusty, might be hidden amongst the trees, and softly weathered timber benches set an interesting backdrop for a collection of pots.

Modern minimalist gardens may feature the simple lines of a Japanese lantern or a contemporary sculpture constructed of shiny metal or polished stone. Unadorned urns and pots with the striking forms of agave and other architectural plants are pieces of art in their own right.

Almost anything can be used to adorn our gardens and provide points of interest – some art can be functional as well as decorative. A collection of vintage watering cans scattered around the garden will provide sources of water for those little garden treasures. A collection of old tools, rakes, spades or cloches can be used to adorn an old shed wall. Beautiful willow trellises or obelisks could support plants in the vegetable garden.

With a little bit of imagination you can utilise almost anything to decorate a garden, be it formal or whimsical, rustic or minimalist. Let your favourite piece of sculpture define the style and setting of your garden.

ART AND SCULPTURE

The formal garden

Single species planting, straight lines and geometric patterns all lend themselves to a formal garden design. Evergreen hedging to emphasise container beds, symmetrical borders and strict linear design offer the balance and form essential to these classic gardens. Structured landscapes often include topiaries, espaliers and containers with a limited number of different plants. All of these elements send a clear and concise structural message in any formal garden.

The common structure of the urban backyard is perfect for a formal approach. **Long narrow** blocks offer an effective way to design a formal garden with garden 'rooms'. The plot can be broken up into sections, or rooms, by using **hedging** or walls to **divide** and **contain** these sections. This offers the gardener an opportunity to conceal **surprises** or changes in colours and plantings between the rooms. The walls also offer **protection** and privacy in an urban setting.

THE FORMAL GARDEN

Although many formal plantings seem perpetually green and lacklustre to flower lovers, it is possible to introduce seasonal interest with container beds filled with spring flowering bulbs followed by mass planting of summer flowering perennials.

Instead of using traditional box topiary, one could quite happily train a flowering climber such as clematis or wisteria into a more formal shape – taming the typically wild tendrils while enjoying the advantage of their spectacular blooms.

Hedging or espaliering camellias will offer a soft, beautifully flowering option for screens and partitions.

Graceful classic statues and busts are commonly used in a formal garden to soften symmetrical borders. Use urns, fountains and other formal containers to frame entrances or make dramatic focal points at the end of pathways and centres of gardens.

As the formal approach is based on traditional garden practices, this style of design is best suited to classic architecture and period-style homes.

Plants for the formal garden

Buxus sempervirens
    (common box) [1]

Camellia sasanqua [2]

Carpinus betulus
    (European hornbeam)

Ficus pumila
    (creeping fig)

Gardenia augusta

Ilex
    (holly)

Ilex crenata
    (Japanese holly)

Juniperus virginiana 'Spartan'

Laurus nobilis
    (bay)

Lavandula spp.

Myrtus communis
    (common myrtle)

Ophiopogon japonicus

Rosa spp. [3]

Rosemarinus spp.

Taxus baccata
    (yew)

Tulipa spp. [4]

The cottage garden

Most often associated with the typical English garden, the cottage garden abounds with whimsy and colour – often in stark contrast with the more formal classic gardens found throughout Europe.

The **design** elements in a **cottage garden** take on a whole new perspective when compared to the formal approach. Instead of relying on symmetry and strict framework, the cottage garden can be any size or shape. Instead of progression planting, **textures**, plant heights, **colours** and **form** are used to create the cottage garden.

Often an **informal mix** of annuals and perennials grown amongst **traditional** roses, the cottage garden style is used in contrast to the single species planting found in formal gardens.

The cottage garden is often full and abundant, carrying an air of romance. Full, heady scents of old-fashioned roses, intense shades of magentas, rich reds, yellows, blues and oranges and the lushness of fresh, green foliage epitomise the romance and profusion of the cottage garden.

*I*nstead of long, lineal walkways, paths meander between garden spaces, inviting visitors into a welcome and peaceful space to discover delights hidden amongst the lush undergrowth. Paths can be paved with old bricks, stones or simply gravel, anything unstructured that blends sympathetically with the surrounding planting. Lawn paths can be used to seamlessly join grassy areas throughout the garden.

Almost anything can be used as a feature in a cottage garden as long as the lines are not too structured. Delicate and informal shapes and pieces that are decorative as well as functional, such as collections of well-used watering cans beside wicker chairs, will all contribute beautifully to the whimsy of the cottage garden.

THE COTTAGE GARDEN

When considering structures in the garden one can use beautifully painted wood or wicker furniture in bright colours that complement the surrounding planting. An arbour creating a romantic walkway or peaceful place to sit can be covered with pendulous blooms to soften its form.

THE COTTAGE GARDEN

Plants for the cottage garden

Alcea rosea (hollyhock) [1]
Alchemilla mollis (lady's mantle)
Anemone x hybrida (Japanese windflower) [2]
Aquilegia x hybrida
Campanula spp. [3]
Clematis montana [4]
Cleome hassleriana
Cosmos bipinnatus (cosmos)
Dahlia spp. [5]
Delphinium x elata hybrids
Dianthus barbatus (sweet William)
Digitalis purpurea (foxglove) [6]
Echinacea purpurea
Gladiolus spp.
Lathyrus odoratus (sweet pea)
Leucanthemum x superbum (shasta daisy)
Lobelia erinus
Matthiola incana (stock)
Nigella damascena (love-in-a-mist)
Phlox drummondii (annual phlox)
Primula vulgaris [7]
Rosa spp.

The container garden

Whether it is a specimen of potted *Acer palmatum* (Japanese maple), an urn filled with a cascading campanula or a prized collection of *Primula auricula* (rockery primrose), no garden feels complete without some sort of containered planting.

From a pair of potted topiary box framing an entrance or terracotta pots filled with spring bulbs, the choices for a container garden are endless. The beauty is in always being able to fill a lonely space in the garden with colour at any time of the year, by rotating potted annuals and bulbs when in full bloom. You can rearrange and replace pots as needed and have a perpetually perfect garden. Even if you have no earth in which to plant, you can still have a glorious green oasis. Patios, rooftops and courtyards can be filled with colour and foliage throughout the year with the container garden.

THE CONTAINER GARDEN

THE CONTAINER GARDEN

There is an unending choice of containers to use in the potted garden. Just the wide variety of shapes and sizes of terracotta and glazed ceramics offers enough choice for most without looking into alternative options such as found or recycled objects. As long as the object provides enough drainage for your plants you can use almost anything – from wheelbarrows to old baths, copper tubs to antique milk vats.

An otherwise uninteresting spot in the garden can be greatly enhanced by a collection of pots clustered together, as long as the type of containers and plant choices complement the surrounding planting. Ends of pathways and entrances offer perfect places for a pair of potted shrubs or a matching set of glorious urns filled with potted colour.

THE CONTAINER GARDEN

The container garden can be a **simple pot** of flowers or a lush **collection** of beauties. Gardeners who have a prized collection of plants can **show** them off to their **full advantage** in a potted garden. The perfect example is a collection of P*rimula auricula*, traditionally displayed as a collection of individual terracotta pots **grouped** together on shelves or terraces. A potted collection of **rare bulbs** can take **centre stage** when in full flower and then be hidden away when lying dormant.

Plants for the container garden

Acer palmatum
   (Japanese maple)

Agave spp.

Aloe bromii

Buxus sempervirens
   (common box)

Cyclamen spp.

Fuchsia spp. [1]

Hosta spp.

Hydrangea spp. [2]

Impatiens spp.

Lavandula spp.

Lewisia spp. [3]

Lobelia spp.

Orchid spp.

Petuna x hybrida

Primula auricula [4]

Primula vulgaris [5]

Sempervivum spp.

Taxus baccata
   (yew)

Tulipa spp.

The contemporary garden

Gardens are most successful when their style complements the surrounding architecture and environment, and with the current trend towards contemporary, modern design of houses, many gardens have also evolved towards a more simple-structured formality, with a minimalist and low-maintenance approach.

The contemporary garden has the air of a formal garden but with a less traditional approach to planting. Instead of using the softer lines of box hedging, the contemporary gardener utilises the mass planting of architectural plants such as flax, which lends a more dramatic impact to the formality. Structural and decorative features also take on a more dramatic edge with the use of exciting new materials and special surface treatments.

The contemporary garden also offers an opportunity for experimenting with new ideas. Garden shows and expos are wonderful forums for designers to compete with each other to create amazing garden spaces with refreshing new concepts on container gardening, walling, sculptures, outdoor furniture or planting ideas.

THE CONTEMPORARY GARDEN

Planting in the contemporary garden almost always involves a strong structural emphasis – whether creating impact with single species planting or using individual plants with distinct architectural value such as phormium, yuccas and bamboos.

Ecologically aware planting has also contributed to the contemporary garden. In these times of low rainfall, modern gardeners are using more drought-tolerant plants, which are often also low maintenance.

Water is also an important element in the contemporary garden. From ponds to fountains, there are many choices available for water features.

There are no rules to follow when using sculpture and art in the contemporary garden and many finishes and materials can be utilised – from concrete to polished stainless steel, rusted metals to carved wood, bronze and coppers through to glass or ceramics.

Contemporary garden designs are ever evolving and gardeners continually come up with new ideas and concepts.

The objective is to see what appeals to you and what works within the available space, and to enjoy the creative freedom that the contemporary garden allows.

Plants for the contemporary garden

Acanthus mollis (bear's breech)
Agave spp. [1]
Aloe arborescens
Carex spp.
Cordyline fruticose
Cotoneaster horizontalis
Cupressus sempervirens (Italian cypress)
Cycas revolute (sago palm)
Hedera helix (English ivy)
Kniphofia spp.
Liriope muscari (lily turf) [2]
Pelargonium benamobra [3]
Phormium tenax (flax)
Phyllostachys utilis (green bamboo)
Sedum 'Purple Emperor' [4]
Stipa gigantea (giant feather grass)
Strelitzia nicolai (bird of paradise)
Trachycarpus fortunei (Chinese windmill palm)
Yucca gloriosa (Adam's needle)

The artist's garden

*I*f gardens are expressions of our souls, then the artist's garden provides a dynamic and passionate expression of the artist's soul. In the following pages we illustrate the art and gardens of some wonderful artists. By looking at their gardens and their art, we gain insight into the personality of the artist.

Most artists' gardens incorporate various forms of sculpture, from metal to stone, and ceramics to mosaics. These pieces may be of a practical nature, such as water features, pots or mirrors or they might be purely decorative pieces that add dimension and form to the garden.

The artist's garden will often be in keeping with their art. Many similarities in shape and feel will exist between the two. If an artist tends to work with more modern materials and finishes, then the garden will usually tend towards a more modern, minimalist feel with straighter lines and more severe planting.

Ceramic artists will sometimes have a more earthy feel to their gardens. Their gardens might utilise more natural features such as bare earth pathways, mossy clearings and asymmetrical garden beds. The planting will also be more wild and whimsical.

THE ARTIST'S GARDEN

Mosaic artists may use a lot of **colour** in their gardens with planting – perhaps using **sunny** borders with a **cacophony** of colour throughout the seasons. Of course, all artists' gardens are **different** and all offer an amazing **insight** into the minds of their creators.

Gardens containing art will often create strong feelings of comfort or discomfort, safety, vulnerability, creativity or wonder in the viewer. This depth of feeling is commonly experienced in beautiful gardens, but when a gardener's own art is incorporated, the feeling can be intensified.

THE ARTIST'S GARDEN

The spiritual garden

A feeling of oneness with the garden – being aligned with nature and one's environment – is the essence of the spiritual garden. It is also about contemplation of the forces and energies of nature. The spiritual garden will often offer visitors a place of pause for meditation or thought. This essence can be captured in large or small gardens, courtyards, patios and even balconies. They can all become still spaces for the spiritual garden

Developing areas within a garden for contemplation is important – areas that create an ambience of tranquillity and serenity, where one can sit and feel the life and movement of the garden, a space to devote time to study the beauty and integrity of nature.

Water is an integral part of the spiritual garden. The movement of water in streams and fountains encourages energy flow through the garden, helping create a tranquil ambience.

The Japanese garden evokes feelings of serenity. The approach to Japanese gardens is one of reverence for the beauty of nature. The use of spirit houses and temples further enhances the spiritual feel of the Japanese garden.

The use of spiritual symbolism and deities, stone Buddhas, temple houses or otherworldly creatures such as fairies can also enhance the spiritual feel of a garden. It is preferable if the owner of the garden has a connection with the symbolic pieces that they choose to use.

THE SPIRITUAL GARDEN

The spiritual garden is an extension of the spiritual essence of the gardener. It is important that the sense of tranquillity and peace feels authentic to the person creating it, as it will often be a spot of healing and contemplation for them alone.

Whatever style one chooses to use in the garden, a spiritual essence can always be evoked. By having a clear intention of what you want to create, you can bring a feeling of tranquillity and peace to any space, be it only a small structure, seat or arbour to sit and contemplate, a water feature that invites the visitor to linger and enjoy the calming effects of the falling water or a simple Zen-inspired stone garden. One only needs to create a connection with nature to bring a spiritual essence to the garden – where a visitor not only enjoys the beauty of the garden, but also the feeling and the energy of the life force of the garden and the surrounding environment.

The woodland garden

Although many gardeners feel perplexed when planning a garden in the shade, it is possible to create interest and beauty in every setting. It is also common for these gardens to become a favourite spot to linger; they are often a space of peace and tranquillity. The woodland garden is a perfect choice for a shaded plot that doesn't get too dry through the summer months. Today's woodland garden is a re-creation of the beautiful forests of North America and Europe. These lush green forests conceal a multitude of magnificent species of flowering perennials and bulbs.

The woodland garden is home to a informal array of plants carpeting the ground beneath lichen-covered tree trunks and dainty flower heads bobbing in the breeze, warmed by dappled sunlight peeping through the canopy above. This varied collection of perennials, bulbs and shrubs echoes the landscape

of the northern forests with their contained wilderness. There might be bulbs naturalising throughout the garden and drifts of groundcovers cascading over edges or creeping along pathways. But there is always a certain amount of planning behind creating this haphazard appearance.

THE WOODLAND GARDEN

*I*n winter, a nourishing layer of leaf mulch hiding the newly forming growth of the early spring bulbs covers the woodland floor. The graceful forms of deciduous trees frame and exhibit the bones of the garden. The poised and beautiful snowdrops, which grow wild throughout Europe, poke their heads from amid the foliage of anemones. These two species, planted in drifts throughout the woodland floor, are a wonderful companion for the flowering winter rose, *Helleborus x hybridus*, a must for any shade garden.

THE WOODLAND GARDEN

As spring approaches more bulbs begin to emerge. The winter aconite and narcissus make an early appearance, their shining yellow blooms herald the blaze of spring to come. Winter flowering shrubs such as H*amamelis mollis* (witch-hazel), *Corylopsis* and mahonia reflect the yellow with their winter blooms.

When the enchantment of spring and summer arrives in the woodland garden, drifts of forget-me-nots edge paths and fill the empty spaces on the woodland floor. Narcissus species continue to appear as do the delicate nodding heads of E*rythronium* and other special bulbs that naturalise beautifully in moist, woodland conditions. Anemones create swathes of white and pale blue. Primulas and scilla also provide a tapestry of white, blues and yellows.

THE WOODLAND GARDEN

Plants for the woodland garden

Actea rubra [1]
Anemone nemorosa (wood anemone)
Arum italicum (Italian arum)
Aruncus doicus
Astrantia major
Bergenia cordifolia
Brunnera macrophylla
Convallaria majalis (lily-of-the-valley)
Corydalis flexuosa
Dicentra formosa
Dicentra spectabilis (bleeding heart)
Digitalis ferruginea (foxglove)
Epimedium davidii
Erythronium californicum [2]
Erythronium dens-canis (dog's tooth violet)
Galanthus ssp. (snowdrop)
Hellborus x hybridus [3]
Hosta spp.
Kirengeshoma palmata
Omphaloides cappadocia
Polygonatum x hybridum (Solomon's seal)
Primula japonica [4]
Primula vulgaris (English primrose)
Pulmonaria spp. (lungwort)
Symphytum 'Goldsmith'
Trillium chloropetalum
Trillium rivale [5]
Uvularia grandiflora
Viburnum macrocephalum [6]

The kitchen garden

Apart from being a practical way of using land, the kitchen garden can also be delightfully decorative – from the walled predecessors of the French potage garden to today's eclectic mix of vegetables, herbs, flowers and art.

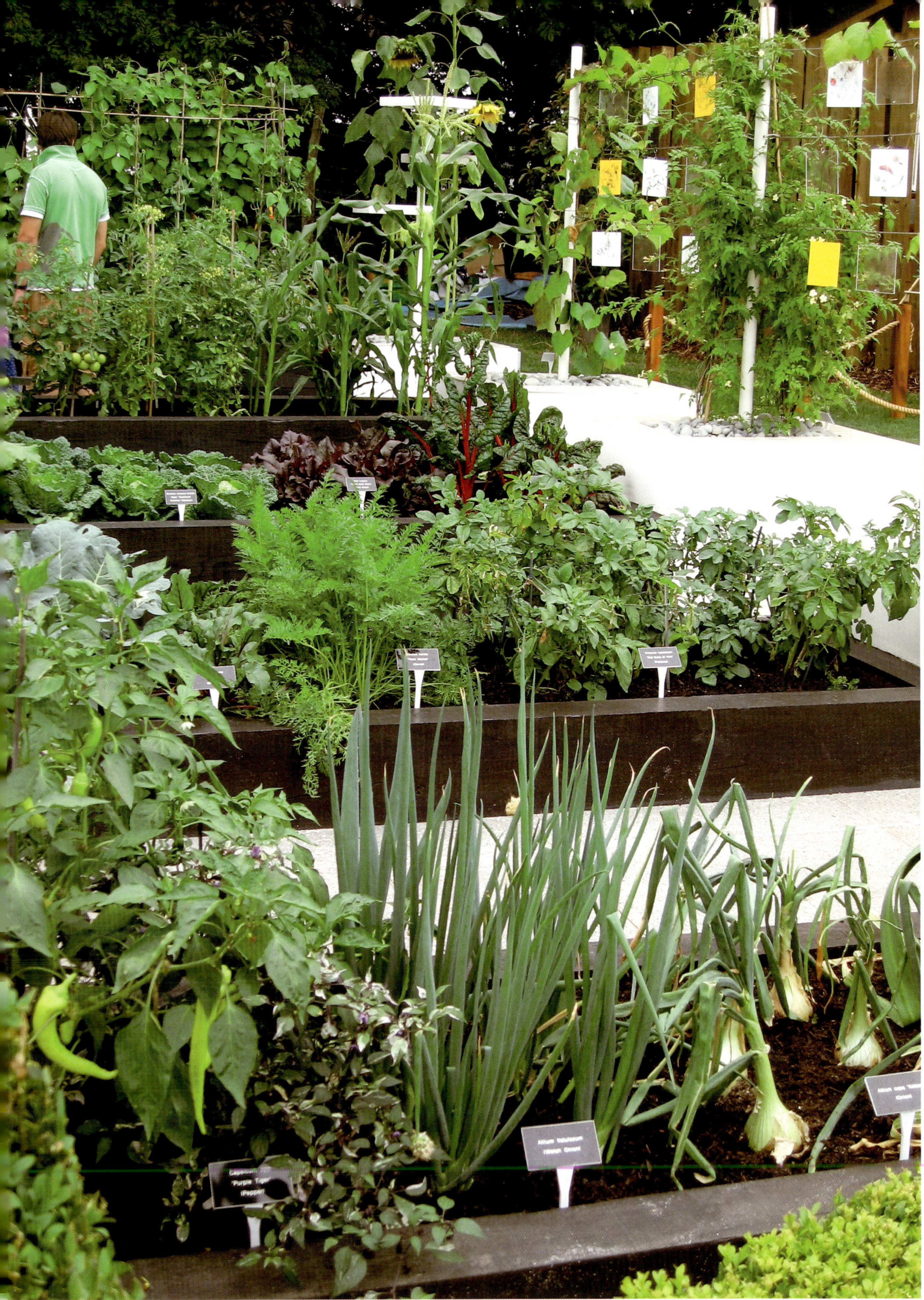
'Purple Tiger'
(Pepper)
Allium fistulosum
(Welsh Onion)

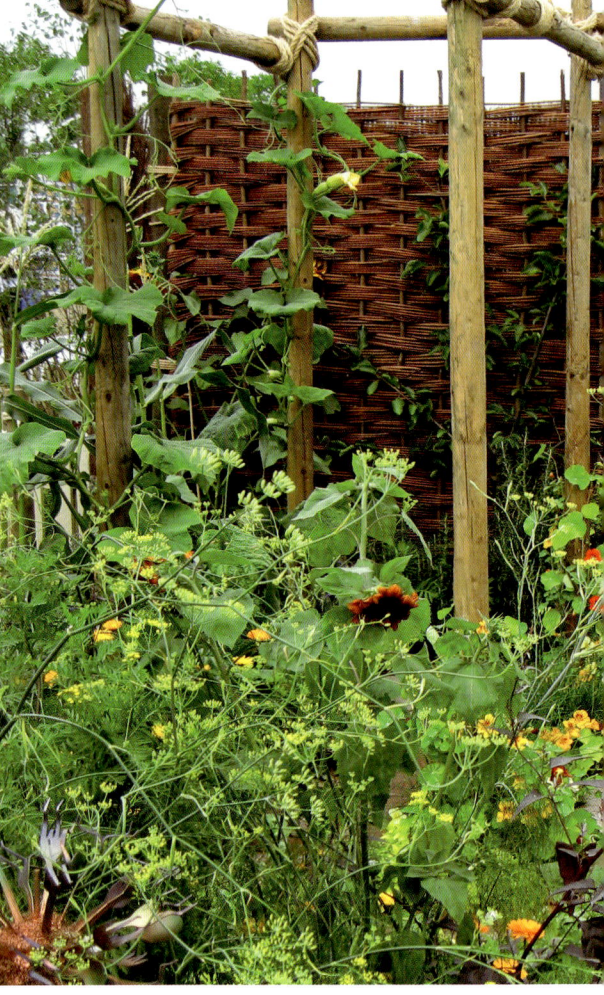

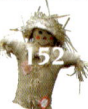

Plots can vary in shape and proportion, but more often than not take on the straight angles of the rectangle; the best proportion being at least one-and-a-half times as long as it is wide. Paths may divide beds and also add to the character of the plot. Formal paving, bordered with tightly clipped hedging adds a very formal and traditional air to the kitchen garden.

The **whimsy** of the romantic cottage garden can be recreated with just a gravel **path** and a **white picket fence** entrance. A mixed **array** of colourful annuals and perennials between the rows of carefully planted seedlings will further **enhance** the exuberance of the **country vegetable garden**.

The style of many of today's kitchen gardens originated from the delightful and diverse French potages. Whether formal or romantic, potages appeared in many shapes and sizes, often as rectangular walled plots. The potages started out walled or at least partially enclosed to protect the vegetables from harsh winds and to create favourable microclimates. With the romantic potage, vegetables are interplanted with green manures or with herbs and flowers and today, as the popularity of decorative gardens grows, many imitate this tried and tested method of companion planting.

THE KITCHEN GARDEN

A wide range of benefits is attributed to growing annuals and perennials in the vegetable garden; certain flowers stimulate growth of vegetables, some protect against pests and diseases and others attract beneficial insects, such as bees, for cross pollination. Some taller flowering plants provide light shade for newly planted seedlings and other deep-rooting varieties provide the benefit of loosening the soil. Above all, they provide a point of beauty and interest in a garden that is most often visited daily throughout the growing season.

THE KITCHEN GARDEN

With the classical-style kitchen garden, each bed is usually divided from the rest with hedging or edgers. Here, the beautiful geometry of the vegetable garden is evident as the eye is drawn along the strictly ordered paths and plots, carefully aligned and lovingly tended. The creative gardener will appreciate the ability to establish different schemes in each bed. Colour schemes are seemingly the obvious choice for those wanting to beautify the space, but practical issues may divide the beds, those being watering preferences or subsistence gardening methods.

THE KITCHEN GARDEN

The water garden

Water features provide wonderful opportunities to create romantic and serene spots to linger in gardens. The comforting presence of a water feature can be felt as soon as you enter a space.

There is nothing quite as beautiful as sitting by a stone-edged stream running into a small pond – the water rimmed by marginal water-loving plants such as primula and iris, the colours of which are reflected in the water's calm surface. You can enjoy listening to the musical overtures of water cascading over carefully placed rocks – the source of the water hidden by overflowing lush green foliage – and watching the movement of the water as insects break its surface. Goldfish lazily glide beneath the water, sometimes hidden by lilies or other graceful water plants that partially cover the surface of the pond.

THE WATER GARDEN

A water garden might be as **simple** as a small **stone water feature** hiding in the undergrowth, the subtle **music** of the falling water **just audible** as you pass in your meanderings through the garden.

Whatever the choice of feature, water is an invaluable addition to any garden. The movement of water in streams and fountains encourages energy flow through the garden, helping to create a feeling of closeness to nature as it enhances and enriches the surrounding environment. It cools the air, reflects movement and colour and creates a constant source of sound.

THE WATER GARDEN

Water can play a role in any garden, regardless of size or budget. The size and structure of the water feature will depend on the size and available space of the site you are working with, so it is important to consider the scale of the water feature you intend to use.

THE WATER GARDEN

The simplest features built with available materials are often the most beautiful. Small ponds lined with local stone, each positioned to give an impression of natural outcroppings, or an abandoned copper tub and other recycled items are all stunning examples of materials that anyone can use to create their own water garden.

THE WATER GARDEN

The bog garden

Any moist situation in a garden can be an ideal spot to plant a bog garden. Whether it is the edge of a stream or pond, or just a damp spot with moisture-retentive soils, there is a wonderful array of colours and textures that can be utilised in your planting. Ligularia, astilbes, primulas, hostas and euphorbias are just a few of the wonderful plants that thrive in these conditions.

The most magnificent specimen that flourishes in these moist conditions is *Gunnera manicata*, which has giant bristly leaves that sometimes reach up to a metre in size and will thrive as long as it is not exposed to full hot sun or intense cold winters. Also grown mostly for their foliage, but on a smaller scale, are the different forms of *Rogersia*, *Rheum* and hostas.

$\mathcal{C}$are must be taken to consider the scale of some of these plants when planning the bog garden.

Bog gardens are a fantastic way of **softening** stream or pool **edges** where garden beds need to seamlessly **blend** in with the wetter areas. They are also great for spots where poor **drainage** or a **high water table** pose problematic planting situations or when a site is underwater for most of the year.

THE BOG GARDEN

A wonderful selection of trees, shrubs and perennials thrive in moist conditions. There is also a choice of wildflower meadow plantings or woodland plantings under shady conditions, but most of the bog plants prefer a constant damp soil rather than waterlogged soil. So consider turning those extra damp areas into a natural water feature and using the waterlogged soil for plants such as marsh marigold or water iris. Bog plants can then be utilised where the soil becomes less waterlogged.

THE BOG GARDEN

When choosing plants for the bog garden, be sure to consider the existing landscape and garden style. The plants should complement surrounding garden beds and water features.

Plants for the bog garden

Carex spp.
Eupatorium purpureum
Euphorbia palustris
Gunnera spp.
Iris ensata
  (Japanese iris) [1]
Iris pseudacorus
Ligularia dentata [2]
Lobelia cardinalis
  (cardinal flower)
Lysichiton americanum
  (skunk cabbage) [3]
Lysimachia clethroides
  (loosestrife)
Petasites japonicus [4]
Primula bulleyana
Primula japonica [5]
Rogersia spp.
Zantedeschia aethiopica
  (arum lily)

The dry garden

Due to climatic changes and times of low rainfall, the drought-tolerant or dry garden has become a very popular choice, and is the only option in some regions. Far from being limited in terms of plant choice, a plethora of plants grow and thrive in these conditions.

*A*part from hot sunny areas, drought-tolerant plants can also come from areas where moisture is hard to get, such as cliff faces, mountain regions and semi-desert regions. Alpine and rockery plants thrive in these conditions as long as they have a good amount of sunlight and good drainage. Few drought-tolerant plants tolerate moisture-retentive soils, so good drainage is essential. Raised beds and sunny rockery gardens are ideal.

Plants that originate from the Mediterranean region and other hot, dry regions such as Australia and South Africa are all worth considering; these exotic plants offer a wonderful variety of form and function for the dry garden.

THE DRY GARDEN

Succulents are valued for their varieties of form and their ease of maintenance; they are a perfect choice for any dry garden. They are also easy to propagate and look good throughout the year.

*L*arger, more architectural plants such as yuccas and agaves should be used as focal plants in a border or utilised as accents in large urns or pots. Smaller terracotta pots look wonderful filled with clusters of sempervivum or stunning flowering aloes. An entire container garden can look wonderful filled with succulents or cacti.

When designing borders for the dry garden there are many different plants to choose from. Varied species of kniphofia flower throughout the year, their colour palette going from lime-yellows through to strong oranges and reds. There are also miniature forms of the kniphofia as well as the more common taller forms to offer variety in their position throughout the border.

Another useful plant to offer contrast with foliage colour and form is the euphorbia. It ranges from lime-green or bronze flowering ground covers through to large, tree-like forms, such as Euphorbia *canariensis*.

Sedums such as *Sedum* 'Autumn Joy' are glorious when mass planted in borders. In summer their lush foliage is invaluable as a backdrop for other plants and their mass of flowers changes from pink through to rust in late autumn.

Many grasses are drought tolerant and can offer a way to soften a dry border with their flowing forms – a beautiful contrast to the strong lines and form of many succulents.

Plants for the dry garden

Aeonium arboreum
Agave atrovirens [1]
Agave spp.
Aloe arborescens
(aloe)
Aloe polyphylla
(spiral aloe) [2]
Carnegiea gigantea
(giant saguaro)
Centaurea montana
(mountain bluet)
Coreopsis spp.
Crataegus spp.
Echeveria elegans
(hens and chickens)
Echinacea purpurea
Echinocactus grusonii
(golden barrel cactus) [3]
Euphorbia spp. [4]
Kniphofia spp. [5]
Protea 'Buckingham Celsissima' [6]
Sansevieria trifasciata
(mother-in-law's tongue)
Sedum spp.
Sempervivum spp.
Stachys byzantina
(lamb's ears)
Strelitzia nicolai
(bird of paradise)
Yucca gloriosa
(Adam's needle)

The bulb garden

Bulbs are one of nature's more brilliant creations, and they provide much variety and pleasure to the gardener. Some of the world's most beautiful flowers bloom from the humble bulb. Bulbs can be used in massed formal planting or naturalised under trees in a more romantic setting. They can accent a well-designed border or fill pots in a small container garden. Although recognised as an integral part of the spring garden, bulbs can be enjoyed throughout the seasons and in most climatic regions.

The blooming of the humble daffodil heralds the arrival of spring. There are so many different varieties of daffodil to choose from that one could never get bored; the flowering season lasts many weeks.

A dramatic feature of **mass-planted tulips** or hyacinths is almost unrivalled for **visual impact**. Interplanting with **annuals** such as pansies or violets can **soften** this look, and the annuals can also **disguise** any aging **bulb foliage**. Annuals are perfect for this, as they will reappear each year with little or no assistance.

When choosing companions for bulbs, whether perennial or annual, always choose flower and foliage colours that complement each other and the surrounding planting, and group bulbs and companions that have similar bloom times.

Surrounding bulbs with a groundcover is a great way to show them off. The groundcover acts as a backdrop for the flowers and offers interest when the bulbs have died down. Early spring combinations such as white primula interplanted with white anemones or English bluebells are a divine choice for the garden.

Shrubs are also great companions to plant back with bulbs – the yellows of the forsythia create a brilliant backdrop for spring daffodils in whites, creams and yellows. The foliage colour of shrubs can also be a contributing factor when planning complementary colour schemes.

Areas underneath deciduous trees can be livened up with the planting of bulbs. The lush, green foliage of an oak tree starting to sprout will contrast beautifully with the blues of mass-planted grape hyacinth at its base.

*L*arge lawns or grassy areas can be transformed with a delightful abundance of colour with naturalised sweeps of spring or autumn bulbs. Crocus, cyclamen, snowdrops and some fritillaries are perfect for naturalising in these conditions as long as they don't have to compete with thick grasses.

Plants for the bulb garden

Allium spp. [1]
Anemone nemorosa (wood anemone)
Convallaria majalis (lily-of-the-valley)
Crocosmia x crocosmiiflora
Crocus spp. [2]
Cyclamen spp.
Eucomis comosa (pineapple lily) [3]
Erythronium dens-canis (dog's tooth violet)
Freesia spp.
Fritillaria meleagris (snake's head fritillary)
Galanthus spp. [4]
Galtonia candicans (summer hyacinth)
Gladiolus spp.
Hyacinthus orientalis (hyacinth)
Hyacinthoides non-scripta (bluebell)
Lilium spp.
Muscari armeniacum (grape hyacinth) [5]
Narcissus spp. [6]
Nerine spp. [7]
Polianthes tuberosa (tuberose)
Ranunculus asiaticus (ranunculus)
Scilla spp.
Trillium chloropetalum
Trillium grandiflorum (wake-robin)
Tulipa spp. [8]

The summer garden

Summer is a season full of passion and energy when gardeners are spoilt for choice with colour and form. Vibrant colour schemes often include mesmerising mixes of crimsons, scarlets, oranges and yellows. Borders might be filled with bursting perennials interplanted with masses of annuals. The summer sun shines down and highlights the contrasts in colour, its warmth heightening the heady scents of the season.

After the exuberance of spring, the fullness and depth of summer is ready to be enjoyed. There are rich, deep tones of foliage and flower. Bold clumps of perennials reach their peak and are ready to burst forth with colour. The warm air gives rise to the lush scents of the garden and there are long days in which to enjoy meandering through the glories of summer planting.

In sunny patches, the gardener gets to enjoy the gloriously big blooms of lilies and oriental poppies in myriad colours. Brilliant globes of alliums look magnificent planted en masse in between perennials in the summer border. Stunning spikes of lupins and delphiniums and the powerful scent of roses, sweet peas, lilacs and honeysuckles will draw in birds and bees alike.

For the shade lover there is the arrival of the glorious hydrangea, blooming in countless shades of pinks, blues and whites. The nodding heads of aquilegias continue, whose invaluable blue-green foliage has graced the garden throughout spring. As the hostas begin to unfurl, a new palette of greens is on offer, the perfect foliage plant for any fertile shady spot.

Although spring is the focal time for bulbs, summer also offers a wonderful choice. The stunning alliums, liliums, galtonias, crinums and gladioli are just a few. As the season progresses, dahlias arrive and offer a dramatic colour palette and impressive stature that fills the garden when many other perennials have finished their flowering. Their blooms seamlessly blend from pink to apricot, through to vibrant oranges, deep reds and moody purples.

THE SUMMER GARDEN

Roses are essential to the midsummer garden; no other plant rivals them for their depth of colour and their sumptuous scents. Roses are tough and hardy but do need a lot of attention to look their best. But they are always worth the effort.

As summer progresses, some early flowering perennials will offer a second burst of colour, grasses are at their prime and attractive seed heads of perennials that haven't been cut back may offer a more muted tone to the border. Hydrangeas continue to flower and will start to change colour once the cooler nights begin to arrive.

Plants for the summer garden

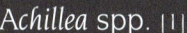

Achillea spp. [1]
Agapanthus spp.
Allium christophii [2]
Allium giganteum
Consolida ambigua (larkspur)
Crambe cordifolia
Eucomis comosa (pineapple lily) [3]
Gladiolus spp.
Hedychium (ginger lily)
Hydrangea macrophylla
Hydrangea paniculata [4]
Iris siberica [5]
Iris spp.
Knifophia spp. [6]
Lilium longiflorum
Lupinus spp.
Myrtus luma (myrtle)
Philadelphus 'Belle Etoile'
Polianthes tuberosa (tuberose)
Rhodohypoxis baurii (rose grass)
Rosa spp.
Verbascum spp.
Viburnum plicatum 'Summer Snowflake'

The autumn garden

*I*t is leaves, rather than flowers, that provide brilliance of colour in the autumn garden. As the cooler weather approaches, trees and plants begin their transformation. With a backdrop of green from surrounding evergreens, deciduous trees and shrubs show off their crimsons and oranges, golds and reds. The vibrancy of the colours of autumn is a delight to behold. Many of the glorious plants that flower in late summer last through autumn, though the hues are more subdued than the colours of summer. Dahlias continue to flower, as do some salvias, rudbekias and penstemons.

Grasses are an invaluable addition to the autumnal garden, their fluffy flower heads rise above everything else and sway gracefully in the wind. The flower heads of grasses and seed heads of summer perennials often hang on through autumn and offer an architectural element to the garden throughout the winter months.

THE AUTUMN GARDEN 215

When looking for shrubs and deciduous trees for autumn colour, one cannot go past *Cotinus* for its brilliance. *Cotinus* 'Grace' offers divine dark-purple

foliage throughout spring and summer, and in autumn this transforms into a deep luminous red. *Enkianthus* also offers an intense red that is almost unrivalled.

Many climbers also offer brilliance in their reds and oranges – *Vitis*, Boston ivy and silver lace creeper, just to name a few.

There are also a few bulbs that bloom in the autumn months. The scented trumpet blooms of the belladonna lily arrive in autumn and provide the garden with one of the longest flowering bulbs. There is also an autumn flowering crocus, *Crocus sativus*, or saffron crocus, and resembling the crocus is *Colchicum autumnale*, or naked ladies. There are also nerines and forms of *Leucojum*, *Scilla* and *Lilium* that flower in the autumn months.

THE AUTUMN GARDEN

Apart from flowers and foliage there is also a choice of fruiting trees, shrubs and plants that offer interest throughout autumn. The bright red berries of the A*rum italicum* replace the often-undistinguished dark leaves of summer. The bright amber berries of the V*iburnum opulus* last several weeks and offer a feast to local birds. As winter approaches, the berries of the hawthorn provide stunning interest to their newly bare branches. It is also the time that hips start appearing on certain rose bushes, some turning from deep reds to black as the season progresses.

Plants for the autumn garden

Acer japonicum 'Aconitifolium' [1]
Acer palmatum
Aconitum carmichaelii
Amaryllis belladonna
Aster novae-angliae
Callicarpa bodinieri var. giraldii 'Profusion'
Colchicum autumnale
Cotinus 'Grace'
Crocus sativus
Cyclamen hederifolium
Dahlia spp.
Enkianthus campanulatus [2]
Eryngium proteiflorum
Euonymus europaeus
Euphorbia dulcis 'Chameleon'

Hamamelis mollis (witch-hazel) [3]
Hydrangea quercifolia (oak leaf hydrangea) [4]
Leucojum autumnal
Liriope muscari [5]
Lycoris radiata
Miscanthus sinensis
Nerine bowdenii [6]
Parthenocissus quinquefolia (Virginia creeper) [7]
Sedum 'Autumn Joy' [8]
Sternbergia lutea
Vitis coignetiae (crimson glory vine)
Vitis vinifera 'Purpurea'

The winter garden

Many gardeners dread the arrival of the winter months, perhaps under the misapprehension that there is a shortage or even a complete absence of colour and interest during this time. It can, however, be a season filled with charm, colour and excitement with its dramatic contrasts, enchanting surprises and quiet grace. The delights of winter abound: there is magic in the mornings when the stark white of a frost covers the garden, clinging to the branches and accentuating each blade of grass.

When the winter colours do appear, it is a dramatic sight that excites the senses. The clear bright yellows of the delightful bulb, winter aconite, the pure whites of giant magnolia flowers and the passionate purples and blacks of hellebores are all magnificent features of winter.

One must also appreciate the **form** and **structure** of the winter garden to understand and perceive its **beauty**, as any garden can look beautiful in the splendour of spring and summer. The winter months **reveal** the 'bones' of the garden and this form is the **building block** for the rest of the year.

THE WINTER GARDEN

The changes in the winter garden are, unlike the frenzy of spring and summer, quite slow. Witness the quiet unfurling of the winter bulbs from beneath the layer of leaf mulch, the gradual blooming of the different forms of hellebores and the slow but graceful arrival of the pendulous blooms of the philbert.

Winter bulbs are an absolute delight. The whites of the various forms of Galanthus (snowdrop) and Leucojum (snowflake), the bright yellow of Eranthis hyemalis (winter aconite) and the soothing lilac shades of Chionodoxa (glory of the snow) are all true winter flowering bulbs. Many other late-winter to early-spring bulbs grace gardens at this time of year. There are enough species of crocus to enjoy this bulb from autumn through to spring, as well as early flowering narcissus, hyacinths, muscari and scilla.

Of the perennials that flower in the winter, none come close to the beauty and diversity of the hellebores. Flowering through all of winter and lasting well into spring, colours range from greens to spotted pinks, pure whites and purples through to almost black.

THE WINTER GARDEN 233

Using flowering shrubs in the winter garden is a must; there is a multitude of choices – from the brazen yellow flowers of forsythia to the alluring oranges of the witch-hazel. Finally, no winter garden is complete without the divine scent of daphne, and who can resist the dramatic whites and pinks of a magnolia in flower?

Plants for the winter garden

Acacia baileyana
Alyogyne huegelii
Berberis thunbergii atropurpurea 'Rose Glow'
Bergenia cordifolia
Chaenomeles x superba 'Coral Sea'
Chimonanthus praecox
Chionodoxa luciliae
(glory of the snow)
Cornus alba 'Elegantissima'
Cornus stolonifera 'Flaviramea'
Corylopsis pauciflora
Corylus avellana 'Contorta'
(contorted filbert) [1]
Crocus spp.

Cyclamen spp.
Eranthis hyemalis
(winter aconite) [2]
Euonymus fortunei 'Emerald 'n Gold'
Galanthus spp.
(snowdrop) [3]
Hamamelis mollis
(witch-hazel)
Hellborus x hybridus [4]
Helleborus niger [5]
Magnolia spp. [6]
Mahonia japonica 'Bealei'
Mahonia x media 'Winter Sun'
Sarcococca ruscifolia

The spring garden

The luminous blues of the first bluebells, the intense greens of unfurling new foliage and the sunny yellows of narcissus all proclaim the arrival of spring. So suited to this time of year is the welcoming brightness of yellow in all its different variations, from its palest lemons to vivid golds and oranges. These yellows sit beautifully back with the spring greens whose brief brilliance fades as spring melds its way into summer.

The glorious mix of colour in spring transforms almost daily; these rapid changes are echoed in the variance of the spring weather.

Along with this arrival of colour, many more perennials that have been lying dormant begin to emerge from the warming earth as do the fresh green sprouts of deciduous shrubs and trees – this intense green is unrivalled throughout the rest of the seasons.

THE SPRING GARDEN

The long hibernation of spring bulbs is finally over as they burst into colour at the first hint of warmth in the air. The first blues, pinks and white of the bluebells are a

delight to the senses. Their soft tones sit beautifully against the pale but clear pinks and white of surrounding blossom trees. The intense yellows of daffodils can often overshadow these pale tones so care must be taken to plan where bulbs are planted.

As the bulbs emerge, this is a most delightful time to play with colour. Try massing intense red tulips with deep orange wallflowers; their brilliant warm tones are a welcome arrival to spring. Experiment with a less potent mix of lilac tulips mixed with yellow and orange ranunculus,

or a contrasting mix of orange tulips massed with blue muscari. Another approach could be a peaceful combination of yellow and white narcissus against the bright yellows of a rhododendron. The colour combinations are endless and all the more powerful when massed.

The **flowers** of spring bulbs and shrubs are usually **short lived** so planning a succession of **overlapping** colours in the spring garden will make the most of this bountiful time. Choosing a colour scheme or schemes and working with that throughout the season is important if you want to create a certain feel or **ambiance** in the garden. For example, early in the season start a colour scheme of **whites** and **yellows** and as spring moves on, continue the yellows and introduce warmer tones with **purples** and **apricots**. This theme can be transformed again later by phasing out the yellows and moving towards the introduction of **pinks** and **reds** to sit back with the purples. This colour combination can then step easily from spring to summer.

THE SPRING GARDEN

Plants for the spring garden

Arum italicum
(Italian arum)
Brunnera macrophylla
Digitalis purpurea 'Alba' [1]
Euphorbia amygdaloides var. robbiae
Euphorbia myrsinites
Forsythia x intermedia 'Spectabilis'
Fritillaria meleagris
(snake's head fritillary)
Hyacinthus orientalis
(hyacinth)
Lunaria annua 'Alba Variegata'
(variegated honesty)
Magnolia salicifolia
Malus 'Gorgeous'
(flowering crab apple) [2]

Muscari spp. [3]
Narcissus spp.
Prunus serrulata
(flowering cherry)
Pulmonaria spp.
Ranunculus asiaticus
Rhododendron spp. [4]
Scilla siberica
Spirea 'Arguta'
Syringa 'Esther Staley'
(lilac)
Tulipa spp. [5]
Viburnum plicatum [6]
Weigela florida

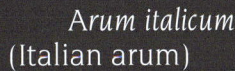

Credits

Thank you to all the garden owners for allowing me to photograph their beautiful gardens.

This credit list does not fully represent all the gardens featured in this book. A small number of owners requested their gardens be credited. I have also credited gardens that are public or in an open garden scheme. All other gardens are not named to provide privacy for the owners.

Garden names are shown in inverted commas
Artists' names are shown without inverted commas
L = left; R = right; C = centre

Climbers
p. 38		'Tieve Tara'
p. 40		'Tieve Tara'
p. 43	(L)	'Tieve Tara'
p. 45	(L)	'Cloud Hill'
	(R)	'Tieve Tara'

Borders
p. 50	(top R)	'Garden of St Earth'
	(bottom)	'Cloud Hill'
p. 51	(bottom)	'Tieve Tara'
p. 52	(bottom L)	'The Garden Vineyard'
p. 53	(bottom R)	'Cloud Hill'
p. 54	(top)	'Cloud Hill'
p. 55	(top)	'Tieve Tara'
	(bottom)	'Cloud Hill'

Stone
pp. 56–57		'Bakery Walk Trentham'
p. 58	(bottom R)	Mim Beaumont

Structure
p. 64	(top L)	'Belafesson'
p. 66		'Tieve Tara'
p. 67		'Glen Rannoch'
p. 71	(C R)	'Tanderra'

Art and sculpture
pp. 72–73		'Tanderra'
p. 74	(top)	Bruno Torfs
p. 76	(top L)	Dianne Barton
	(top R)	Jo Heriot
	(bottom L)	Jo Heriot
p. 77		Charlie Aquilina

The formal garden
pp. 80–81		'Ballantrae'
pp. 82–83	(top C)	'Cloud Hill'
p. 85	(top C)	'Cloud Hill'

The cottage garden
p. 94	(L)	'Tieve Tara'
	(R)	'Belafesson'
p. 95	(R)	'Belafesson'
p. 99	(L)	'Ballantrae'
	(R)	'Belafesson'

The container garden
p. 106	(L)	'Cloud Hill'
pp. 106–107	(C)	Shades of Gray

The contemporary garden
p. 116		Charlie Aquilina
p. 119	(top R)	Dianne Barton

The artist's garden
pp. 122–123		Shades of Gray
p. 124	(top L)	Charlie Aquilina
	(top C)	Bruno Torfs
	(top R)	Dianne Barton
	(bottom L)	Shades of Gray
	(bottom C)	Bruno Torfs
	(bottom R)	Shades of Gray
p. 125	(top)	Bruno Torfs
	(bottom)	Dianne Barton
p. 126	(L)	Shades of Gray
		Charlie Aquilina
p. 127	(L)	Bruno Torfs
		Dianne Barton
p. 128		Jenny Aquilina
p. 129		Shades of Gray
pp. 130–131		Shades of Gray

The spiritual garden
p. 134	(L)	'Forest Glade'
p. 138		'Forest Glade'

The woodland garden
p. 147	(top L)	'Alton'
	(bottom)	'Dreamthorpe'
p. 148		'Dreamthorpe'

The kitchen garden
pp. 150–151		'Heronswood'
p. 154	(top)	'Belafesson'
p. 155		'Tugurium'
pp. 156–157	(bottom)	'Tugurium'

The water garden
p. 164	(C)	'Ballantrae'
p. 166	(L)	'Cloud Hill'
p. 168	(bottom)	'Cloud Hill'

The bog garden
pp. 170–171		'Tieve Tara'
p. 174		'Tieve Tara'
p. 178	(bottom L)	'Tugurium'

The bulb garden
p. 195	(bottom)	'Duniera'
p. 196	(bottom)	'Ballantrae'
p. 197	(L)	'Ballantrae'

The summer garden
pp. 200–201		'Garden of St Earth'
p. 202	(R)	'Tieve Tara'
pp. 204–205		'Tieve Tara'
p. 206	(bottom)	'Tieve Tara'
p. 210	(top)	'Glen Rannoch'
	(bottom)	'Garden of St Earth'

The autumn garden
p. 215	(R)	'Tieve Tara'
p. 219		'Forest Glade'
p. 221	(bottom R)	'Forest Glade'
p. 222	(bottom)	'Bolobek'

The winter garden
p. 226	(L)	'Alton'
p. 228		'Glen Rannoch'
p. 229		'Glen Rannoch'
p. 230		'Duniera'
p. 233	(top R)	'Tieve Tara'
		'Forest Glade'

The spring garden
p. 238		'Glen Rannoch'
p. 240		'Duniera'
p. 241	(L)	'Forest Glade'
p. 242	(bottom L)	'Ballantrae'
	(bottom C)	'Ballantrae'

INDEX

Acacia baileyana	235
Acanthus mollis (bear's breech)	121
Acer japonicum 'Aconitifolium'	223
Acer palmatum (Japanese maple)	103, 111, 223
Achillea spp.	211
Achillea 'Moonshine'	21
Aconitum carmichaelii	223
Actea rubra	149
Actinidia (kiwifruit)	47
Adam's needle	see *Yucca gloriosa*
Aeonium arboreum	189
Agapanthus spp.	211
Agapanthus campanulatus	26
Agave spp.	121, 189, 111, 185
Agave atrovirens	189
Ajuga reptans 'Catlin's Giant'	35
Akebia quinata (chocolate vine)	47
Alcea rosea (hollyhock)	101
Alchemilla mollis (lady's mantle)	101
Allium spp.	199, 202, 207
Allium christophii	25, 211
Allium giganteum	25, 207, 211
Aloe spp.	185
Aloe arborescens	121, 189
Aloe bromii	111
Aloe polyphylla (spiral aloe)	189
Alyogyne huegelii	235
Amaryllis belladonna	221, 223
Anemone hupehensis (Japanese windflower)	20, 51
Anemone nemorosa (wood anemone)	149, 199
Anemone nemorosa 'Vestal'	20
Anemone x hybrida (Japanese windflower)	101
Angelica gigas	27
annual phlox	see *Phlox drummondii*
Antirrhinum 'Liberty Crimson' (snapdragon)	23
Aquilegia spp.	35
Aquilegia longissima	21
Aquilegia vulgaris 'Nora Barlow'	24
Aquilegia x hybrida	101
Artemisia absinthium (common wormwood)	30, 35
Arum italicum (Italian arum)	149, 222, 247
Arum italicum 'Marmoratum'	35
arum lily	see *Zantedeschia aethiopica*
Aruncus doicus	149
Aster novae-angliae	223
Astilbe spp.	23, 24, 171
Astrantia major	149
Astrantia major 'Roma'	24
bamboo	117
bay	see *Laurus nobilis*
bear's breech	see *Acanthus mollis*
Begonia 'Clips'	23
bellflower	see *Campanula persicifolia* 'Alba'
Bellis perennis 'Pomponette'	24
Berberis thunbergii 'Red Pillar'	35
Berberis thunbergii atropurpurea 'Rose Glow'	235
Bergenia spp.	35
Bergenia cordifolia	149, 235
bird of paradise	see *Strelitzia nicolai*
black mondo	see *Ophiopogon planiscapus* 'Nigrescens'
bleeding heart	see *Dicentra spectabilis*
bluebell	see *Hyacinthoides non-scripta*
Boston ivy	see *Parthenocissus tricuspidata*
Bougainvillea spp.	47
Brunnera macrophylla	34, 149, 247
Buddleja davidii 'Black Knight'	25
Buxus sempervirens (common box)	89, 111
Cactaceae (cacti)	185
cacti	see Cactaceae
Calendula 'Indian Prince'	22
California poppy	see *Eschscholzia* 'Orange King'
Californian bluebell	see *Nemophila menziesii* 'Penny Black'
Callicarpa bodinieri var. *giraldii* 'Profusion'	223
Callistephus chinensis 'Lilliput Blue Moon'	27
Camellia spp.	87
Camellia japonica 'Julia Drayton'	23
Camellia sasanqua	89
Campanula spp.	25, 101
Campanula persicifolia 'Alba' (bellflower)	20
Canna spp.	35
Canna x ehemanii	23
Canna x generalis	22
cardinal flower	see *Lobelia cardinalis*
Carex spp.	121, 179
Carnegiea gigantea (giant saguaro)	189
Carpinus betulus (European hornbeam)	89
castor oil plant	see *Ricinus communis* 'Impala'
Centaurea cyanus (cornflower)	26
Centaurea montana (mountain bluet)	26, 189
Centranthus ruber (valerian)	24
Cerinthe major	26
Chaenomeles x superba 'Coral Sea'	235
Chilean bellflower	see *Lapageria rosea*
Chilean jasmine	see *Mandevilla sanderei*
Chimonanthus praecox	235
Chinese windmill palm	see *Trachycarpus fortunei*
Chionodoxa luciliae (glory of the snow)	232, 235
chocolate cosmos	see *Cosmos atrosanguineus*
chocolate vine	see *Akebia quinata*
Cimicifuga simplex 'Brunette'	32, 35
Clematis spp.	24, 44
Clematis 'Jackmanii'	25
Clematis montana	20, 47, 101
Cleome hassleriana	101
climbing hydrangea	see *Hydrangea petiolaris*
Cobaea scandens	25
Colchicum autumnale	221, 223
common box	see *Buxus sempervirens*
common myrtle	see *Myrtus communis*
common wormwood	see *Artemisia absinthium*
Consolida ambigua (larkspur)	211
Consolida ambigua 'Imperial Series'	25
Consolida ambigua 'Rosamond'	24
Continus 'Grace'	218
contorted filbert	see *Corylus avellana* 'Contorta'
Convallaria majalis (lily of the valley)	20, 149, 199
Cordyline fruticose	121
Coreopsis spp.	189
Coreopsis tinctorial	21
Coreopsis verticillata	21
cornflower	see *Centaurea cyanus*
Cornus alba 'Elegantissima'	235
Cornus mas 'Variegata'	34
Cornus stolonifera 'Flaviramea'	235
Corydalis flexuosa	26, 149
Corylopsis spp.	146
Corylopsis pauciflora	235
Corylus avellana 'Contorta' (contorted filbert)	235
Cosmos atrosanguineus (chocolate cosmos)	27
Cosmos bipinnatus (cosmos)	24, 101
Cosmos bipinnatus 'Sonata White'	20
cosmos	see *Cosmos bipinnatus*
Cotinus 'Grace'	218, 223
Cotinus coggygria 'Royal Purple'	32, 35
Cotoneaster horizontalis	121
Crambe cordifolia	211
Crataegus spp.	189
creeping fig	see *Ficus pumila*
crimson glory vine	see *Vitis coignetiae*
Crinum spp.	207
Crocosmia 'Lucifer'	23, 35
Crocosmia x crocosmiiflora	22, 199
Crocus spp.	198, 199, 221, 235
Crocus sativus	221, 223
Cupressus sempervirens (Italian cypress)	121
Cycas revolute (sago palm)	121
Cyclamen spp.	35, 111, 198, 199, 235
Cyclamen hederifolium	223
daffodil	see *Narcissus* spp.
Dahlia spp.	101, 203, 213
Dahlia 'Biddenham Sunset'	22
Dahlia 'Bishop of Llandaff'	23, 35
Dahlia 'Grenadier'	23
Dahlia 'Lavender Athalie'	24
Dahlia 'Pearl of Heemstede'	24
Dahlia 'Requiem'	25
Dahlia 'Sure Thing'	23
Dahlia coccinea	22
day lily	see *Hemerocallis citrina*
Delphinium 'Black Knight'	25
Delphinium elatum 'Blue Nile'	26
Delphinium spp.	202
Delphinium x elata hybrids	101
Dianthus 'Doris'	24
Dianthus barbatus (sweet William)	101
Dianthus barbatus 'Nigrescens'	27
Dicentra formosa	149
Dicentra spectabilis (bleeding heart)	149

Dicentra spectabilis 'Alba'	20	
Digitalis ferruginea (foxglove)	149	
Digitalis purpurea (foxglove)	24	
Digitalis purpurea 'Alba'	20, 247	
dog's tooth violet	see Erythronium dens-canis	
Echeveria elegans (hens and chickens)	189	
Echinacea purpurea	24, 101, 189	
Echinocactus grusonii (golden barrel cactus)	189	
Echium spp.	26	
English ivy	see Hedera helix	
English lavender	see Lavandula angustifolia	
English primrose	see Primula vulgaris	
Enkianthus spp.	218	
Enkianthus campanulatus	223	
Epimedium spp.	35	
Epimedium davidii	149	
Eranthis hyemalis (winter aconite)	21, 232, 235	
Eremurus 'Cleopatra'	22	
Eryngium alpinum	26	
Eryngium proteiflorum	223	
Erysimum wheeleri	22	
Erythronium spp.	146	
Erythronium californicum	149	
Erythronium dens-canis (dog's tooth violet)	149, 199	
Erythronium pagoda	21	
Eschscholzia 'Inferno'	22	
Eschscholzia 'Orange King' (California poppy)	22	
Eucomis comosa (pineapple lily)	199, 211	
Euonymus fortunei 'Emerald 'n Gold'	235	
Euonymus europaeus	223	
Eupatorium purpureum	25, 179	
Euphorbia spp.	35, 171, 186, 189	
Euphorbia amygdaloides var. robbiae	247	
Euphorbia canariensis	186	
Euphorbia dulcis 'Chameleon'	27, 32, 223	
Euphorbia griffithii 'Dixter'	22	
Euphorbia myrsinites	247	
Euphorbia palustris	179	
European hornbeam	see Carpinus betulus	
Ficus pumila (creeping fig)	89	
Filipendula rubra	24	
flax	see Phormium tenax	
flowering cherry	see Prunus serrulata	
flowering crab apple	see Malus 'Gorgeous'	
Forsythia spp.	21, 196, 234	
Forsythia x intermedia 'Spectabilis'	247	
foxglove	see Digitalis ferruginea and Digitalis purpurea	
Freesia spp.	199	
Fritillaria spp.	198	
Fritillaria meleagris (snake's head fritillary)	199, 247	
Fritillaria persica	27	
Fuchsia spp.	111	
Galanthus spp. (snowdrop)	149, 198, 199, 232, 235	
Galtonia spp.	207	
Galtonia candicans (summer hyacinth)	20, 199	
Gardenia augusta	89	
Geranium himalayense 'Gravetye'	25	
giant feather grass	see Stipa gigantea	
giant saguaro	see Carnegiea gigantea	
ginger lily	see Hedychium	
Gladiolus spp.	101, 199, 207, 211	
Gladiolus 'Jo Wagenaar'	23	
glory of the snow	see Chionodoxa luciliae	
golden barrel cactus	see Echinocactus grusonii	
grape hyacinth	see Muscari armeniacum
green bamboo	see Phyllostachys utilis
Gunnera spp.	179
Gunnera manicata	35, 172
Hamamelis mollis (witch-hazel)	146, 223, 234, 235
Hedera helix (English ivy)	121
Hedychium (ginger lily)	211
Helenium 'Waldtraut'	22
Helianthus spp.	21
Hellebrous spp.	226, 231
Hellborus x hybridus	145, 149, 235
Helleborus niger	20, 235
Hemerocallis 'American Revolution'	27
Hemerocallis 'Meadow Sprite'	27
Hemerocallis 'Stafford' (day lily)	23
Hemerocallis citrina (day lily)	21
hens and chickens	see Echeveria elegans
Heuchera spp.	35
holly	see Ilex
hollyhock	see Alcea rosea
honeysuckle	see Lonicera
hops	see Humulus lupulus
Hosta spp.	33, 35, 111, 149, 171, 172
Humulus lupulus (hops)	47
hyacinth	see Hyacinthus orientalis
Hyacinthoides non-scripta (bluebell)	199
Hyacinthus 'Blue Magic'	26
Hyacinthus orientalis (hyacinth)	199, 247
Hydrangea spp.	26, 111, 206
Hydrangea arborescens 'Annabelle'	20
Hydrangea macrophylla 'Blue Wave'	26
Hydrangea macrophylla	211
Hydrangea paniculata	211
Hydrangea petiolaris (climbing hydrangea)	20, 47
Hydrangea quercifolia (oak leaf hydrangea)	20, 223
Iceland poppy	see Papaver nudicaule 'Red Sails'
Ilex (holly)	89
Ilex crenata (Japanese holly)	89
Impatiens spp.	111
Imperator cylindrica rubral (Japanese blood grass)	35
Ipomoea purpurea (morning glory)	26, 47
Iris spp.	163, 211
Iris 'Night Owl'	25
Iris chrysographes	27
Iris ensata (Japanese iris)	25, 179
Iris pseudacorus (yellow flag iris)	21, 179
Iris siberica	211
Iris unguicularis (winter iris)	26
Italian arum	see Arum italicum
Italian cypress	see Cupressus sempervirens
Japanese blood grass	see Imperator cylindrica rubral
Japanese holly	see Ilex crenata
Japanese iris	see Iris ensata
Japanese maple	see Acer palmatum
Japanese windflower	see Anemone hupehensis and Anemone x hybrida
Japanese wisteria	see Wisteria floribunda
Juniperus virginiana 'Spartan'	89
Kirengeshoma palmata	149
kiwifruit	see Actinidia
Knautia macedonica	27
Kniphofia spp.	21, 23, 121, 189, 211, 186
lady's mantle	see Alchemilla mollis
lamb's ears	see Stachys spp.
Lamium spp.	35
Lapageria rosea (Chilean bellflower)	23, 47
larkspur	see Consolida ambigua
Lathyrus odoratus (sweet pea)	47, 101, 202
Laurus nobilis (bay)	89
Lavandula spp.	89, 111
Lavandula angustifolia (English lavender)	30, 35
Lavatera trimestris 'Mont Blanc'	20
Lavatera Trimestris 'Silver Cup'	24
Leonotis leonurus	22
Leucanthemum x superbum (shasta daisy)	101
Leucojum spp.	221, 232
Leucojum autumnal	223
Lewisia spp.	111
Ligularia spp.	171
Ligularia 'The Rocket'	21
Ligularia dentata	179
lilac	see Syringa spp.
Lilium spp.	199, 207, 221
Lilium 'Fire King'	22
Lilium candidum	20
Lilium henryi	22
Lilium longiflorum	211
lily of the valley	see Convallaria majalis
lily turf	see Liriope muscari
Linum perenne (perennial flax)	26
Liriope muscari (lily turf)	25, 35, 121, 223
Lithodora diffusa 'Grace Ward'	26
Lobelia spp.	111
Lobelia cardinalis (cardinal flower)	23, 179
Lobelia erinus	101
Lobularia maritima (white alyssum)	20
Lonicera (honeysuckle)	47, 202
loosestrife	see Lysimachia clethroides
love-in-a-mist	see Nigella damascena
Lunaria annua 'Alba Variegata' (variegated honesty)	247
lungwort	see Pulmonaria spp.
Lupinus 'Polar Princess' (white lupin)	20
Lupinus 'The Governor'	25
Lupinus 'Thundercloud'	25
Lupinus spp.	202, 211
Lychnis chalcedonica	23
Lycoris radiata	223
Lysichiton americanum (skunk cabbage)	179
Lysimachia clethroides (loosestrife)	179
Magnolia spp.	234, 235
Magnolia salicifolia	247
Magnolia stellata	20
Mahonia japonica 'Bealei'	235
Mahonia x media 'Winter Sun'	235
Malus 'Gorgeous' (flowering crab apple)	247
Mandevilla sanderei (Chilean jasmine)	47
Matteuccia struthiopteris (shuttlecock fern)	35
Matthiola incana (stock)	101
Meconopsis cambrica (Welsh poppy)	22
Meconopsis grandis	26
Melianthus major	35
Miscanthus sinensis 'Zebrinus' (zebra grass)	33, 35
Miscanthus sinensis	223
morning glory	see Ipomoea purpurea
mother-in-law's tongue	see Sansevieria trifasciata
mountain bluet	see Centaurea montana
Muscari spp.	232, 243, 247
Muscari armeniacum (grape hyacinth)	26, 199

INDEX

myrtle	see Myrtus luma
Myrtus communis (common myrtle)	89
Myrtus luma (myrtle)	211
Narcissus spp. (daffodil)	192, 199, 232, 241, 243, 247
nasturtium	see Tropaeolum majus 'Empress of India'
Nemophila menziesii 'Penny Black' (Californian bluebell)	27
Nerine spp.	199
Nerine 'Fothergilli Major'	23
Nerine bowdenii	223
New Zealand flax	see Phormium tenax 'Purpureum'
Nicotiana sylvestris (tobacco plant)	20
Nigella damascena (love-in-a-mist)	26, 101
Nigella damascena 'Persian Jewels'	20
oak leaf hydrangea	see Hydrangea querciflora
Omphaloides cappadocia	149
Ophiopogon japonicus	89
Ophiopogon planiscapus 'Nigrescens' (black mondo)	32, 35
Orchid spp.	111
oriental poppy	see Papaver orientale 'Harvest Moon'
ornamental millet	see Pennisetum glaucum 'Purple Majesty'
pansy	see Viola tricolor
Papaver nudicaule 'Red Sails' (Iceland poppy)	22
Papaver orientale 'Allegro Viva'	23
Papaver orientale 'Goliath'	23
Papaver orientale 'Harvest Moon' (oriental poppy)	22
Parthenocissus quinquefolia (Virginia creeper)	47, 223
Parthenocissus tricuspidata (Boston ivy)	47
Passiflora caerulae (passionflowers)	47
passionflowers	see Passiflora caerulae
Pelargonium spp.	23
Pelargonium benamobra	121
Pennisetum glaucum 'Purple Majesty' (ornamental millet)	27
Penstemon spp.	213
Penstemon 'Raven'	25
perennial flax	see Linum perenne
Petasites japonicus	179
Petuna x hybrida	111
Philadelphus 'Belle Etoile'	211
Phlox carolina 'Miss Lingard'	20
Phlox drummondii (annual phlox)	101
Phlox paniculate 'Skylight'	24
Phormium spp.	117
Phormium tenax (flax)	121
Phormium tenax 'Purpureum' (New Zealand flax)	32, 35
Phyllostachys utilis (green bamboo)	121
pineapple lily	see Eucomis comosa
Polgonum bistorta 'Superbum'	24
Polianthes tuberosa (tuberose)	199, 211
Polygonatum odoratum (Solomon's seal)	20, 149
Primula spp.	146, 163, 171
Primula auricula	103, 110, 111
Primula bulleyana	21, 179
Primula japonica	149, 179
Primula vulgaris (English primrose)	24, 101, 111, 149
Protea 'Buckingham Celsissima'	189
Prunus serrulata (flowering cherry)	247
Pulmonaria spp. (lungwort)	34, 35, 149, 247
Pulmonaria 'Lewis Palmer'	25
Ranunculus spp.	243
Ranunculus asiaticus (ranunculus)	199, 247
Ranunculus ficaria 'Brazen Hussy'	21

Rheum spp	172
Rhododendron spp.	243, 247
Rhododendron 'Elizabeth'	23
Rhododendron 'Sir Edmund'	24
Rhodohypoxis baurii (rose grass)	211
Ricinus communis 'Impala' (castor oil plant)	23
Rogersia spp.	29, 172, 179
Rodgersia aesculifolia	35
Rodgersia pinnata	35
Rogersia pinnata 'Superba'	24
Rosa spp. (rose)	23, 47, 89, 101, 202, 207, 211
Rosa 'Iceberg'	20
Rosa 'Nuits de Young'	27
Rosa 'Pat Austin'	22
rose grass	see Rhodohypoxis baurii
rose	see Rosa spp.
Rosemarinus spp.	89
Rudbekia spp.	213
Rudbekia hirta	21
sago palm	see Cycas revolute
Salvia spp.	213
Salvia 'Purple Majesty'	25
Salvia patens	26
Salvia viridis	25
Sansevieria trifasciata (mother-in-law's tongue)	189
Sarcococca ruscifolia	235
Scabiosa atropurpurea 'Ace of Spades'	27
Scilla spp.	26, 146, 199, 221, 232
Scilla siberica	247
Sedum spp.	24, 51, 186, 189
Sedum 'Autumn Joy'	35, 186, 223
Sedum 'Purple Emperor'	27, 121
Sempervivum spp.	111, 185, 189
shasta daisy	see Leucanthemum x superbum
shuttlecock fern	see Matteuccia struthiopteris
skunk cabbage	see Lysichiton americanum
Smilacina racemosa	20
snake's head fritillary	see Fritillaria meleagris
snapdragon	see Antirrhnium 'Liberty Crimson'
snowdrop	see Galanthus spp.
Solomon's seal	see Polygonatum odoratum
speedwell	see Veronica prostrata
spiderwort	see Tradescantia 'Blue and Gold'
spiral aloe	see Aloe polyphylla
Spirea 'Arguta'	247
Stachys spp. (lamb's ears)	189
Stachys byzantina	30, 35
star jasmine	see Trachelospermum jasminoides
Sternbergia lutea	223
Stipa gigantea (giant feather grass)	121
stock	see Matthiola incana
Strelitzia nicolai (bird of paradise)	121, 189
Succulents	185
summer hyacinth	see Galtonia candicans
sweet pea	see Lathyrus odoratus
sweet William	see Dianthus barbatus
Symphytum 'Goldsmith'	149
Syringa 'Esther Staley'	24, 247
Syringa spp. (lilac)	202
Taxus baccata (yew)	89, 111
Tellima grandiflora spp.	35
Tiarella spp.	35
Tithonia rotundifolia 'Torch'	22

tobacco plant	see Nicotiana sylvestris
Trachelospermum jasminoides (star jasmine)	47
Trachycarpus fortunei (Chinese windmill palm)	121
Tradescantia 'Blue and Gold' (spiderwort)	26
Tradescantia pallida	27, 35
Trillium chloropetalum	27, 149, 199
Trillium grandiflorum (wake-robin)	199
Trillium rivale	149
Tropaeolum majus 'Empress of India' (nasturtium)	23
tuberose	see Polianthes tuberosa
Tulipa spp.	89, 111, 193, 199, 243, 247
Tulipa 'Black Parrot'	27
Tulipa 'Generaal de Wet'	22
Tulipa 'Golden Apeldoorn'	21
Tulipa 'Ile de France'	23
Tulipa 'Queen of Sheba'	22
Tulipa 'Queen of the Night'	27
Tulipa sprengeri	23
Uvularia grandiflora	149
valerian	see Centranthus ruber
variegated honesty	see Lunaria annua 'Alba Variegata'
Verbascum chaixii 'Gainsborough'	21
Verbascum spp.	30, 211
Veronica prostrata (speedwell)	26
Veronica spicata	26
Viburnum spp.	34
Viburnum macrocephalum	149
Viburnum opulus	222
Viburnum plicatum 'Summer Snowflake'	211
Viburnum plicatum	20, 247
Viola spp. (violet)	193
Viola 'Roscastle Black'	27
Viola tricolor (pansy)	193
violet	see Viola spp.
Virginia creeper	see Parthenocissus quinquefolia
Vitis spp.	220
Vitis coignetiae (crimson glory vine)	42, 47, 223
Vitis vinifera 'Purpurea'	223
wake-robin	see Trillium grandiflorum
Weigela florida	247
Welsh poppy	see Meconopsis cambrica
white alyssum	see Lobularia maritima
white lupin	see Lupinus 'Polar Princess'
winter aconite	see Eranthis hyemalis
winter iris	see Iris unguicularis
Wisteria spp.	43
Wisteria floribunda (Japanese wisteria)	47
Wisteria sinensis 'Alba'	20
Wisteria sinesis	25
witch-hazel	see Hamamelis mollis
wood anemone	see Anemone nemorosa
yellow flag iris	see Iris pseudacorus
yew	see Taxus baccata
Yucca spp.	117, 185
Yucca gloriosa (Adam's needle)	121, 189
Zantedeschia aethiopica (arum lily)	179
zebra grass	see Miscanthus sinensis 'Zebrinus'
Zinnia 'Early Wonder Mixed'	22
Zinnia 'Envy'	23